ÎNSOMNIA CAFÉ™

by M. K. PERKER

Editor...DIANA SCHUTZ
Associate Editor .... DAVE MARSHALL
Digital Production .... MATT DRYER
Design ....JOSH ELLIOTT
Publisher..MIKE RICHARDSON

INSOMNIA CAFÉ™

Published by Dark Horse Books
A division of Dark Horse Comics, Inc.
10956 SE Main Street
Milwaukie, Oregon 97222

darkhorse.com

Library of Congress Cataloging-in-Publication Data

Perker, M. K., 1972-
  Insomnia café : a graphic novel / M.K. Perker. -- 1st ed.
    p. cm.
  ISBN 978-1-59582-357-1
  1. Graphic novels. I. Title.
  PN6727.P464I57 2009
  741.5'973--dc22
                                                    2009021285

First edition: November 2009
ISBN 978-1-59582-357-1

10 9 8 7 6 5 4 3 2 1
Printed in China

INSOMNIA CAFÉ™

story and art
M. K. PERKER

script assist
BRENDAN WRIGHT

lettering
MATT DRYER

DARK HORSE BOOKS®

For Asli.

WOOF!
WOOF!
WOOF!

UHH...

LAIKA!
SHUT UP!
BAD DOG!

LEAVE THE
HOMELESS
MAN
ALONE.

MY
HEAD...

"HOMELESS"? I GUESS
HE'S *TECHNICALLY* RIGHT...
UGHHH...
BETTER CLEAR MY HEAD
BEFORE THE BIG DAY.
COFFEE...

EXCUSE
ME, SIR?

MR. KOLINSKY?
PETER? MAY
WE HAVE
A WORD
WITH YOU?

IT'S ABOUT A CERTAIN
OBJECT. WE'D LIKE YOU
TO ACCOMPANY US TO
A PLACE OF MUTUAL
INTEREST.

" ...PLACE"? WHO
ARE THESE GUYS?
NOT COPS, SO...
SHIT! HOW DID
THEY FIND ME SO
QUICKLY?

HEY!
STOP!

SOMEBODY STOP HIM!

DAMMIT. SHE SAID THERE'D BE CONSEQUENCES.

THAT'S RIGHT-- I WENT THE OTHER WAY.

I NEED COFFEE BEFORE ANYTHING ELSE.

Milano CAFE

HOW THE HELL DID THEY FIND ME? IT'S ONLY BEEN SEVEN, EIGHT HOURS. THEY CAN'T BE COPS. COPS DON'T RANDOMLY GO AFTER THE HOMELESS. THEY SAID THEY'D TAKE ME TO "A *PLACE*," NOT A POLICE STATION.

HI. I'LL HAVE A CUP OF COFFEE. WHERE'S THE RESTROOM?

STRAIGHT AHEAD, ON THE LEFT.

THERE MUST BE SOME KIND OF TRACER--

--SOMETHING HIDDEN IN THE BOOK. HOW ELSE DID THEY FIND ME? WHAT AN IDIOT I AM! WHY DIDN'T I THINK OF IT BEFORE, WITH ALL THOSE VALUABLE BOOKS JUST SITTING ON THE SHELVES?

OF **COURSE** THEY HAVE SOME WAY TO TRACK THEM DOWN. MAYBE IN THE BINDING.

MAYBE **NOT** THE BINDING...

SURE...WHY ELSE MAKE THESE OLD-FASHIONED BOOKMARKS? NO ONE'S SUSPICIOUS OF A BOOKMARK.

CLEVER. NOW WE'LL SEE IF THEY CAN FIND ME.

WHAT THE F--?

BLOOD?!

IT'S BLEEDING? HOW IS THAT **POSSIBLE**? OH, MY GOD...

POLICE! OPEN THE DOOR!

UH...

UH...HOLD ON A SECOND.

OPEN THE GODDAMN DOOR NOW!

I JUST NEED A MOMENT. I'M ... USING THE BATHROOM.

OKAY, I'M UNLOCKING THE DOOR NOW. WHAT'S THE PROBLEM?

HANDS WHERE WE CAN SEE THEM! DON'T DO ANYTHING STUPID!

SIR, STEP OUT THE DOOR. **NOW**. KEEP YOUR HANDS UP.

ALL RIGHT, ALL RIGHT.

GET HIM AGAINST THE WALL. SEE WHAT'S IN THE BRIEFCASE.

DON'T MOVE!

IF THIS IS ABOUT THE TOILET, I WAS GOING TO FLUSH.

SHUT UP.

TAKE A LOOK AROUND. SEE IF THERE'S ANYTHING ELSE.

WHAT IS IT, HARRY?

THE BRIEFCASE ...IT'S FULL OF BLOOD.

LOOK, I CAN EXPLAIN. I MEAN, IF YOU'LL JUST--

FUCK!

WHAT THE HELL IS GOING ON IN THERE?

FUCK!

I'M GONNA ...

...BOOARGH!

SIR, THERE'S...THERE'S...

WHAT?

THERE'S A PAIR OF HANDS IN THE BAG, DETECTIVE BARTELLA, SIR!

HANDS? WHAT THE HELL ARE YOU TALKING ABOUT?

HANDS?

9

TIRED OF TOSSING AND TURNING ALL NIGHT?

THE BACK-O-PEDIC IS DIFFERENT. IT RELIEVES KEY PRESSURE POINTS, HELPING YOU SLEEP BETTER.

WITH OUR SOOTHING SLEEP-NUMBER SYSTEM, THE BACK-O-PEDIC GIVES YOU AND YOUR SWEETHEART A BETTER NIGHT'S REST.

CALL ONE-EIGHT-HUNDRED TWO-ONE-TWO...

I HATE YOU!

SHUT UP, WOMAN!

CALL NOW!

JUST SHUT THE FUCK UP!

I SHOULD BUY YOU IDIOTS THE MATTRESS. THEN MAYBE YOU'LL SLEEP ONE NIGHT FOR A CHANGE.

I'LL KILL YOU!

PLEASE DO.

ONE-EIGHT-HUNDRED TWO-ONE-TWO...

HELLO? BACK-O-PEDIC? HI, UM...I HAVE A QUESTION: DO YOU PERSONALLY HAVE A BACK-O-PEDIC MATTRESS? I MEAN, DO YOU OWN ONE YOURSELF?

HOW IS THAT "IRRELEVANT"? I'M ASKING IF YOU OWN WHAT YOU'RE SELLING.

ENOUGH! I'VE HAD ENOUGH!

NO, THAT'S NOT ME. MY NEIGHBORS ARE TRYING TO KILL EACH OTHER.

NO, THEY *DIDN'T* WAKE ME UP.

YOU LIAR! YOU'RE A FUCKING MONSTER!

SEE, THAT WAS LIKE A BAD JOKE FROM A MEL BROOKS MOVIE, WHERE AN OUTSIDE VOICE CONTRADICTS THE PERSON TALKING--

--HELLO?

HELLO?

I CAN'T BELIEVE SHE HUNG UP ON ME! WHAT'S HER PROBLEM?

SHUT THE FUCK UP!

YOU SHUT THE FUCK UP!

YOU TALKIN' TO **ME**? HUH?

NO, I'M TALKING TO MYSELF, BUT SINCE YOU'RE ALSO ME, THEN YES, I'M TALKING TO YOU.

AND I'M GOING TO KILL MYSELF BY PUTTING THESE BULLETS BETWEEN YOUR EYES! THEN YOU'LL KNOW WHO'S PULLING THE STRINGS!

perker

BUT I'M ALSO PULLING THE STRINGS! WE'RE BOTH PULLING THEM, FROM DIFFERENT ENDS.

STOP! AAGH! STOP IT!

I'M GONNA KILL YOU!

AAH! STOP! AAAHHH!

THE ENERGIZERS PROVIDE THE REMOTE WITH ENERGY. WITHOUT ENERGY, THE REMOTE DOESN'T WORK. IT'S LIKE THE REMOTE'S FOOD...**FOOD**?

NO FUCKING **ANYTHING** IN THE FRIDGE. IT'S 3:00 IN THE MORNING, AND I'M STARVING.

WHERE'D I PUT THOSE TAKEOUT MENUS?

HI, YES, I'D LIKE TO ORDER, UH... ONE LARGE BURRITO AND A COKE. 320 EAST 96TH STREET. APARTMENT 2A. THANK YOU.

SHIT, IT'S ALMOST 4:00 A.M.

OH, NO.

THAT STREET PERSON HAS DOGS. THEY'LL PROBABLY RUN AFTER THE DELIVERY GUY'S BIKE.

THEY'LL SMELL THE FOOD, AND THE DELIVERY GUY WILL NEVER COME BACK.

I'LL HAVE TO SCARE THE DOGS AWAY SOMEHOW.

CRAP, HE'S ALREADY HERE.

BUT HOW--? MAYBE THE BATTERIES...

WOOFFF!

WOOOF! WOF! WOOFF!

13

HEY!

WOOF! WOOF!

WOOF!

WOOF! WOOF! WOOF!

YAAAGH!

FUCK!

WOOF! WOOF!

CRAP. THE BATTERIES "ENERGIZED" THE DOGS. THEY'LL KILL HIM!

HEELP! HEELP!

HEY! YOU **DROP** THAT! THAT'S NOT YOURS!

HEY, I'M TALKING TO YOU!

perker

THAT'S **MY** FUCKING FOOD! I'M DYING UP HERE, GODDAMMIT!

--DOG HAIR, CAT HAIR. IT SWEEPS IT ALL AWAY.

ZZZ...

14

DI-DI-DI

DI-DI-DIT

DI-DI-DI-DIT

MAN, IT'S ALMOST 10:00. I SHOULDN'T HAVE SNOOZED.

CLEAR THE WAY!

YES, SIR, WE INFORMED THE FAMILY. SOMEONE SHOULD BE HERE FOR THE KIDS SOON.

EXCUSE ME, OFFICER. WHAT'S GOING ON?

YOUR NEIGHBOR KILLED HIS WIFE LAST NIGHT AND JUST CALLED 9-1-1.

YOU'RE RIGHT NEXT DOOR. DIDN'T YOU HEAR ANYTHING?

NO, I WAS ASLEEP.

WOW, HE REALLY DID IT THIS TIME. I NEVER THOUGHT HE'D ACTUALLY KILL HER.

MAN, DO I NEED A CUP OF COFFEE. BLACK.

CHAPTER 2

DU PAIN BAKERY

DON'T GET ME WRONG. IT'S JUST THAT WE'RE *DISTRIBUTION*, NOT PUBLISHING. WE'RE ON THE *BUSINESS* SIDE OF THE EQUATION--

--BUT *HE* HAS NO BUSINESS SENSE AT ALL! HE CAN'T EVEN GET UP EARLY.

IS THERE A PROBLEM?

OH, MR. KOLINSKY, YOU FINALLY DECIDED TO SHOW UP. THE MONDAY MEETING IS OVER.

ALL RIGHT, GUYS, LET'S GO.

IT'D BE NICE IF YOU AT LEAST TRIED.

NO, YOU SEE, THIS IS HOW I TAKE MY VACATION: INSTEAD OF THREE WEEKS A YEAR, I TAKE TWO HOURS A DAY, AND IT COMES OUT EVEN.

HEY, PETER?

16

HEY...UM, DO YOU HAVE A COUPLE MINUTES? I MEAN, IF YOU DON'T...

NO, NO, IT'S OKAY, CARLOS. WHAT'S UP?

UM...YOU KNOW....

...A COUPLE WEEKS AGO AT CELIA'S BIRTHDAY PARTY, I...UM...CONFIDED IN YOU ABOUT SOMETHING.

I...UM...I TOLD YOU I WORK FOR THE FBI. NOT DIRECTLY, BUT WITH THE INFRAGUARD.

WELL, IT'S NOT TRUE. I... I LIED TO YOU.

IT'S OKAY, CARLOS. YOU WERE DRUNK.

NO, NO, I'M... I'M SEEING A SHRINK, AND SHE SAID I SHOULD APOLOGIZE TO EVERYONE I'VE LIED TO.

HMM...

OKAY, APOLOGY ACCEPTED.

JUST BETWEEN US, RIGHT?

NO WORRIES, MY FRIEND. WHAT YOU'RE DOING IS VERY BRAVE.

YOU'RE A NOBLE MAN, PETER.

IN CONCLUSION, IF WE DIVIDE THE CITY INTO THREE PARTS--

--THESE TWO PARTS STILL AREN'T COMPARABLE TO THE FIRST ONE.

SO WE'RE FOCUSING ON THE SMALLER BOROUGHS.

ANYTHING YOU WANT TO ADD, MR. HYDEN?

NO, TIM, THAT WAS VERY CLEAR. I THINK THAT'LL DO IT.

THANK YOU VERY MUCH, EVERYBODY.

MR. KOLINSKY, I'D LIKE A WORD WITH YOU.

EVERY TIME YOU'RE IN MY OFFICE, YOU STARE AT THAT PAINTING FOR TEN MINUTES.

18

"AMERICAN GOTHIC" IS MY ALL-TIME FAVORITE.

HOW ABOUT A "CUBAN GOTHIC"? THESE ARE THE FINEST.

CAN WE SMOKE HERE?

IT'S MY BUILDING. I CAN DO WHATEVER THE HELL I WANT.

SO, YOU WERE LATE AGAIN. WHAT THE HELL IS GOING ON?

IS IT A GIRL?

BECAUSE I KNOW YOU DON'T DRINK, AND YOU'RE NOT INTO DRUGS.

YOU'RE RIGHT. I LIKE COFFEE, THOUGH.

I LIKE LIQUOR.

YEAH, I KNOW. YOU DRINK A LOT, AND YOU SMOKE THESE CIGARS EVERY DAY. YOU SHOULD BE CAREFUL, OLD MAN. THIS STUFF'LL KILL YOU.

NO, NO! QUITE THE CONTRARY. DRINKING DOESN'T KILL YOU--

--DRINKING **ALONE** DOES.

HOW ABOUT DRINKING COFFEE ALONE?

PETER... DON'T.

OKAY, I'LL CUT OUT THE CAFFEINE.

DON'T PLAY DUMB WITH ME.

THIS IS YOUR LAST CHANCE. I KNOW YOU DON'T LIKE IT HERE, BUT YOU NEED A JOB.

I WANT YOU HERE ON TIME EVERY MORNING, LIKE EVERYONE ELSE. AS A FRIEND, I WANT THAT FROM YOU.

I'M SORRY. IT WON'T HAPPEN AGAIN.

I DON'T CARE THAT YOU DON'T GIVE A DAMN ABOUT THIS PLACE. WHAT I CARE ABOUT IS YOUR LACK OF GRATITUDE. YOU KNOW MY MOTTO IN LIFE, PETER: "NEVER, EVER IGNORE--"

"NEVER IGNORE A MAN'S COURTESY." I KNOW.

--DOG HAIR, CAT HAIR, LONG HAIR, SHORT HAIR, YOUR HAIR, MY HAIR! ALL SWEPT AWAY BY THIS AMAZING NEW--

THOSE ARE MY CRAYONS!

LITTLE BRATS! THEY'RE GONNA KILL EACH OTHER! FIGHTING MUST BE GENETIC IN THAT FAMILY.

THREE A.M.-- LUNCHTIME.

HI, I'D LIKE TO PLACE AN ORDER...

WHAT DO YOU MEAN YOU WON'T DELIVER? WHAT DOGS? I HAVE NO IDEA WHAT YOU'RE TALKING ABOUT.

YOU FUCKING ASSHOLES! THERE'RE NO DOGS HERE!

I DON'T WANT TO GO OUT AT THIS TIME OF NIGHT, BUT I'LL DIE OF STARVATION HERE.

MAN, SO MANY PEOPLE OUT TONIGHT. IT'S LIKE AN INSOMNIA EPIDEMIC. WHAT DO THEY DO THIS LATE, ANYWAY?

INSOMNIA CAFÉ? THAT SHOULD BE INTERESTING...

HELLO. WOULD YOU LIKE TO SEE OUR SELECTION OF WORLD COFFEES?

I'D LIKE SOMETHING TO EAT.

OUR SANDWICHES ARE REALLY GOOD.

I'LL HAVE A HAM AND CHEESE SANDWICH. AND REGULAR COFFEE.

HERE'S THAT COFFEE. YOUR SANDWICH WILL BE RIGHT UP.

EEUW!

THIS ISN'T COFFEE. IT'S DARK, FOUL WATER. WHERE THE HELL DID THE WAITRESS GO? THERE MUST BE A DESIGNATED BLACK HOLE THEY DISAPPEAR INTO WHEN YOU REALLY NEED THEM.

I CAN'T DRINK THIS. WHAT KIND OF *CAFÉ* IS THIS? IT'S LIKE McDONALD'S WITHOUT BURGERS.

EXCUSE ME? MISS? THIS COFFEE IS *HORRIBLE*.

REALLY?

UM...CAN I GET SOME BAILEY'S IN MY COFFEE?

ARE YOU SURE?

YOU MUST BE SCHIZOPHRENIC. COFFEE WITH BAILEY'S IS A SCHIZOPHRENIC DRINK: "I WANT TO GET DRUNK, BUT I WANT TO STAY AWAKE."

YOU WORK HERE?

NO--

--I WAS PASSING BY AND DECIDED TO STAND BEHIND THE COUNTER AWHILE.

IS THIS YOUR PLACE?

MY-- NO, NO, I...I JUST...

WORK HERE.

SEE, SOMETIMES YOU ASK A LEGITIMATE QUESTION AND GET A SARCASTIC ANSWER.

THEN THE QUESTION SOUNDS STUPID.

THEN YOU'RE FORCED TO ASK A FOLLOW-UP QUESTION, WHICH IS ALSO COMPLETELY LEGITIMATE, BUT THE ANSWER YOU GET IS ACTUALLY THE ANSWER TO YOUR FIRST QUESTION.

HMM.

GO ON . . .

BUT NOW THE PERSON WHO GAVE THE SARCASTIC ANSWER SOUNDS STUPID, THEN THEY REALIZE--

--THAT THE FOLLOW-UP QUESTION WAS ACTUALLY SARCASTIC. AND NO, C&B IS NOT SCHIZOPHRENIC-- COFFEE LATE AT NIGHT IS. C&B AT 3:00 A.M. IS *IRONIC*.

THEN WHY DIDN'T YOU ORDER C&B IN THE FIRST PLACE?

NOW THAT'S A SARCASTIC QUESTION THAT WON'T SOUND STUPID NO MATTER HOW I ANSWER.

COFFEE WITH BAILEY'S, ON THE HOUSE.

HEY, PETER...SOMEBODY CALLED WHILE YOU WERE AT LUNCH. HE SAID HE USED TO WORK WITH YOU AND HE'S IN TOWN FOR A FEW DAYS.

WHAT DID YOU TELL HIM?

HE ASKED FOR YOUR HOME ADDRESS. I SAID I DIDN'T KNOW IT AND TRANSFERRED HIM TO THE FRONT DESK.

THEN SHE SAYS...

EXCUSE ME, CELIA.

I'M SORRY. CARLOS JUST TOLD ME I HAD A PHONE CALL. A MAN CALLED--

YES, A FORMER CO-WORKER OF YOURS. HE SAID HE WANTED TO SURPRISE YOU AND ASKED FOR YOUR ADDRESS.

PETER KOLINSKY.

SHIT!

LONG TIME NO SEE. THOUGHT I'D STOP BY AND SEE HOW YOU'RE DOING. WE SHOULD GET A DRINK.

YEAH, WHAT A NICE SURPRISE...

SHIT! SHIT! SHIT!

CHAPTER
3

WHAT KIND OF A RARE BOOK EXPERT **ARE** YOU? YOU GOT **NOTHING**.

WELL, THE BOOKS ARE **RARE**.

I DON'T LIKE PEOPLE MAKING JOKES WHEN I ASK A NORMAL QUESTION.

SORRY. I QUIT RARE BOOKS.

HOW COULD YOU?

YOU WERE REALLY GOOD. YOU MADE US A LOT OF MONEY.

AND BECAUSE OF IT, I WAS FIRED FROM MY JOB. SO I **HAD** TO QUIT.

DON'T BE SO SENTIMENTAL. CHANGE IS GOOD. NOW LISTEN: I HAVE AN OFFER FOR YOU.

BY THE WAY, THIS COFFEE SUCKS.

WE ACQUIRED A HANDWRITTEN QURAN FROM SYRIA. LOOKS REALLY OLD. I NEED YOU TO CHECK IT OUT FOR ME.

FIGURE OUT WHAT IT'S WORTH-- AND IF IT'S **GENUINE**. YOU CAN'T TRUST **NOBODY** FROM THE MIDDLE EAST.

MR. OBLOMOV, I WAS FIRED FROM ONE OF THE BIGGEST AUCTION HOUSES IN THE COUNTRY BECAUSE OF THE LAST "JOB" I DID FOR YOU. WITH ALL DUE RESPECT, I'M LUCKY I DIDN'T GO TO JAIL.

YOU DIDN'T GO TO JAIL BECAUSE YOU CUT A DEAL WITH THE FEDS-- AND MY BROTHER *DID* GO TO JAIL, BECAUSE, UNLIKE YOU, HE CARES ABOUT LOYALTY. YOU *OWE* ME, AND THIS IS HOW YOU'RE GOING TO PAY ME BACK.

LOOK, MR. OBLOMOV, I FOUND A JOB AT A BOOK DISTRIBUTOR, THANKS TO AN OLD CUSTOMER. I OWE IT TO HIM NOT TO FUCK IT UP.

COFFEE ALWAYS MAKES ME NEED TO PISS. WHERE'S YOUR BATHROOM?

OH, AT THE END OF THE HALLWAY.

THIS WAY? IN THIS DIRECTION?

UM, YES...ON THE RIGHT.

I'M SORRY... WHAT'RE YOU DOING?

I CAN'T HOLD IT ANY LONGER.

NOW, BACK TO BUSINESS. AS I SAID, YOU *DON'T* HAVE AN OPTION. I'M OFFERING YOU A WAY OUT OF YOUR DEBT.

ZZZP!

TOMORROW, 9:00 P.M. YOU KNOW THE PLACE. IF YOU DON'T SHOW UP, I'LL HOLD MY SHIT IN UNTIL MY NEXT VISIT.

28

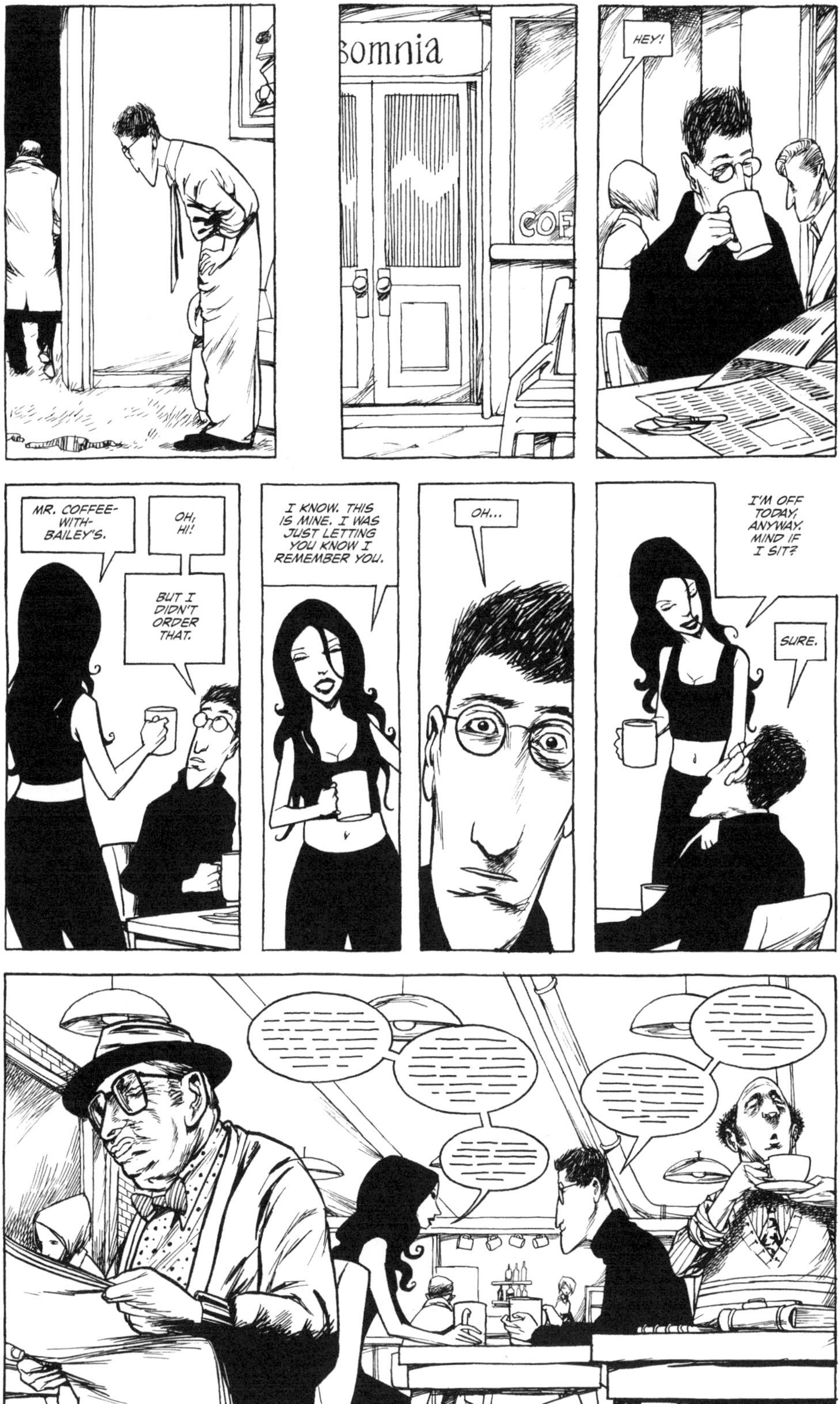
somnia
COF
HEY!
MR. COFFEE-WITH-BAILEY'S.
OH, HI!
BUT I DIDN'T ORDER THAT.
I KNOW. THIS IS MINE. I WAS JUST LETTING YOU KNOW I REMEMBER YOU.
OH...
I'M OFF TODAY, ANYWAY. MIND IF I SIT?
SURE.

WOW, THAT'S ONE HELL OF A STORY!

YEAH . . . WELL, IT'S ALMOST MORNING. I SHOULD GO.

SURE. STORE SHELVES AWAIT YOUR BOOKS.

IT WAS GREAT TALKING TO YOU, ANGELA. I'LL PROBABLY STOP BY AGAIN.

I'LL PROBABLY BE HERE.

PETER!

THEY'RE REALLY PISSED THAT YOU'RE LATE AGAIN. I TOLD THEM YOU HAD A DENTIST APPOINTMENT.

I SAID YOU TOLD ME YESTERDAY, AND YOU HOPED IT WOULDN'T TAKE LONG.

HOLD ON...

PETER, WHERE THE HELL HAVE YOU BEEN? YOU'RE LATE AGAIN.

I WAS AT THE DENTIST, TIM. I TOLD YOU YESTERDAY.

SEE YOU LATER.

NO, YOU DIDN'T. WHICH DENTIST? WHAT'S HIS NAME?

UH...

YOU DON'T BELIEVE ME? HIS NAME IS... DOCTOR...McKEEBY. B.H. McKEEBY.

YOU WANT TO CALL HIM? HERE!

ALL RIGHT, ALL RIGHT. RELAX. JUST BE ON TIME TOMORROW.

UNBELIEVABLE. WHAT'LL IT BE NEXT, A NOTE FROM MY MOTHER? WHAT IS THIS, HIGH SCHOOL?

AH, 3:00 A.M. LUNCHTIME.

I'M STARVING, MONSIEUR. HOW ARE YOU?

NO, MONSIEUR. COFFEE, PLEASE.

WHO ARE YOU TALKING TO?

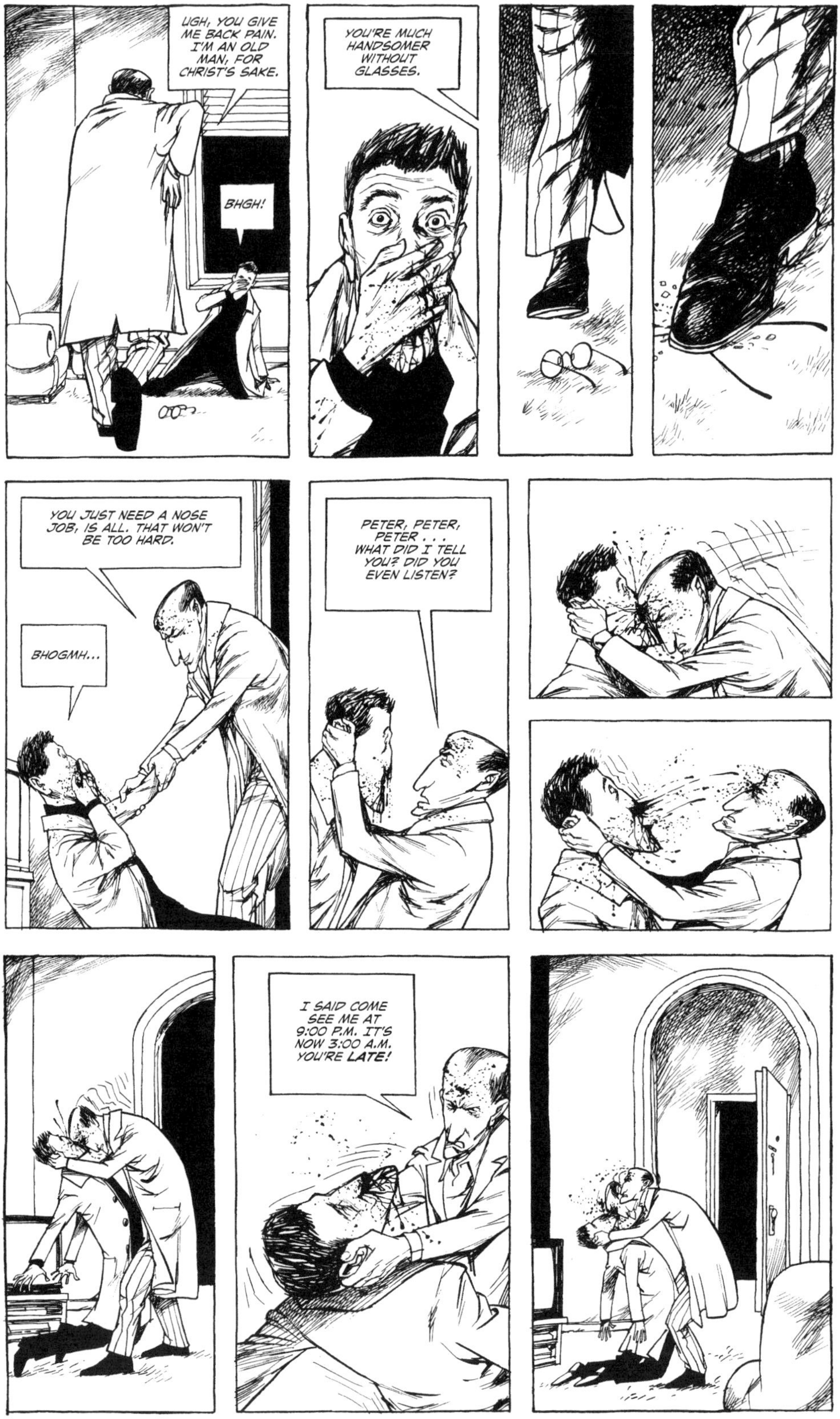
UGH, YOU GIVE ME BACK PAIN. I'M AN OLD MAN, FOR CHRIST'S SAKE.
BHGH!
YOU'RE MUCH HANDSOMER WITHOUT GLASSES.
YOU JUST NEED A NOSE JOB, IS ALL. THAT WON'T BE TOO HARD.
BHOGMH...
PETER, PETER, PETER . . . WHAT DID I TELL YOU? DID YOU EVEN LISTEN?
I SAID COME SEE ME AT 9:00 P.M. IT'S NOW 3:00 A.M. YOU'RE LATE!

CHAPTER
4

COME ON, PETER.
WAKE UP. IT'S
ALMOST 4:00 A.M.

WELL, IF YOU'RE THAT TIRED,
I'LL LET YOU SLEEP.

SWEET
DREAMS.

YOU'LL
CATCH
COLD OUT
HERE,
THOUGH.

GO
TO
BED.

Insomnia

Hi...

CAN I GET A
SKIM LATTE?
EXTRA SHOT,
PLEASE.

SURE.

33

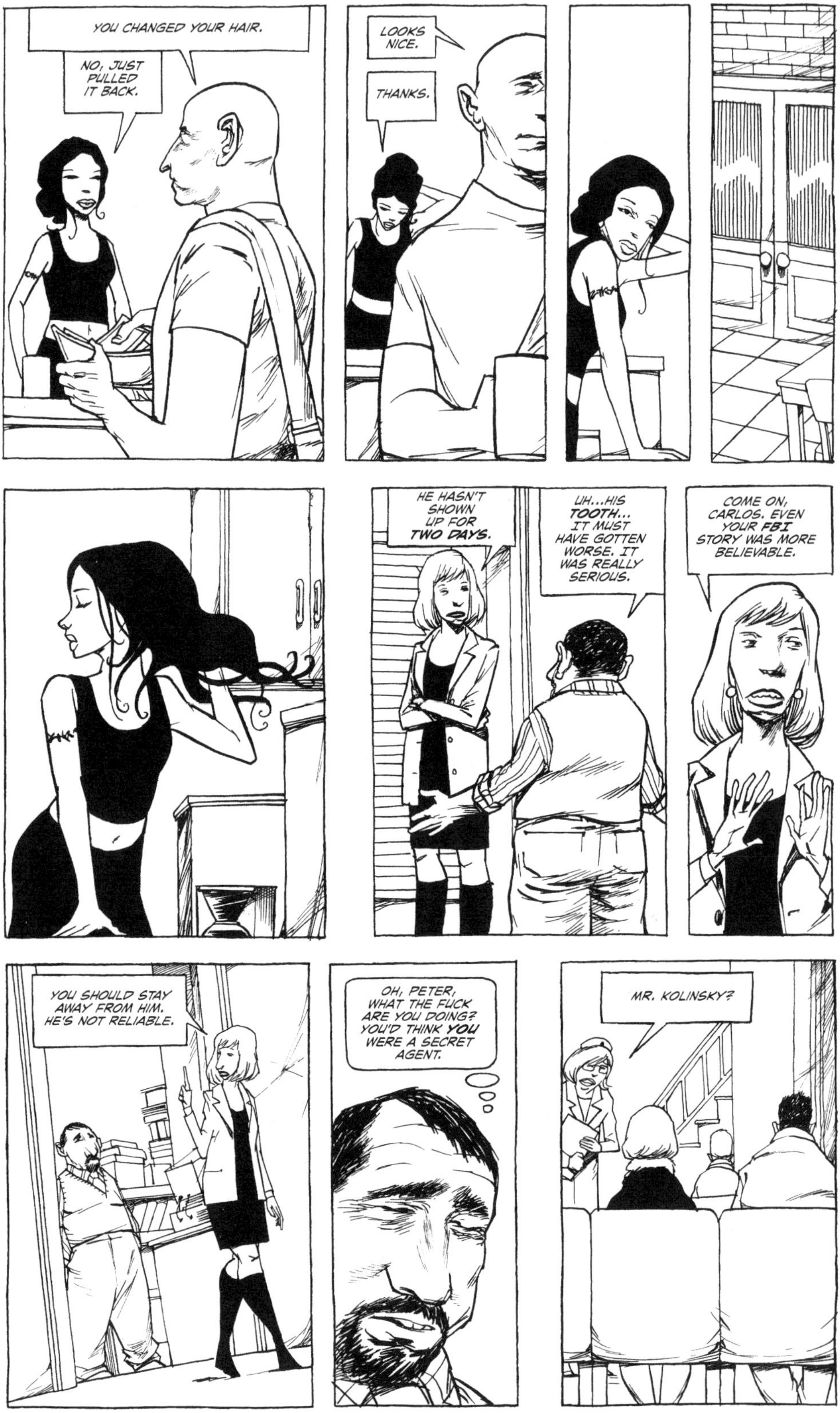
YOU CHANGED YOUR HAIR.
NO, JUST PULLED IT BACK.
LOOKS NICE.
THANKS.
HE HASN'T SHOWN UP FOR TWO DAYS.
UH...HIS TOOTH... IT MUST HAVE GOTTEN WORSE. IT WAS REALLY SERIOUS.
COME ON, CARLOS. EVEN YOUR FBI STORY WAS MORE BELIEVABLE.
YOU SHOULD STAY AWAY FROM HIM. HE'S NOT RELIABLE.
OH, PETER, WHAT THE FUCK ARE YOU DOING? YOU'D THINK YOU WERE A SECRET AGENT.
MR. KOLINSKY?

HMM... HMM... OKAY.

IT'S DIFFICULT TO SLEEP IN YOUR CONDITION, BUT YOU **LOOK** RESTED.

SO, WHAT DID THE COPS SAY? YOU DID GO TO THE **POLICE**, RIGHT?

WELL, IT WAS A HOMELESS GUY. WHAT CAN THE POLICE **DO**, Y'KNOW?

I MEAN, EVERYONE'S COMPLAINING ABOUT THEM LATELY.

YOU CAN'T EVEN GET FOOD DELIVERED AT NIGHT BECAUSE OF THEM.

TO BE HONEST, I'VE NEVER HEARD OF A RANDOM ASSAULT IN WHICH THE ASSAILANT DELIBERATELY HITS THE SAME SPOT OVER AND OVER AGAIN. BUT IT'S UP TO YOU.

MOTHERFUCKERS. MOTHERFUCKING ASSHOLES. SONS OF BITCHES. I FUCKING **HATE** DOCTORS.

insomnia

MA-AN, I'M SO TIRED. MY ANKLES ARE *KILLING* ME.

PSST... ANGELA...

LOOK WHO'S HERE.

HOLY SHIT!

DOES IT HURT?

NO. BUT MY GLASSES ARE BROKEN, SO I CAN'T SEE VERY WELL.

OKAY, I'LL TELL YOU-- --EVERYTHING, FROM THE BEGINNING.

UNTIL A YEAR AGO, I WAS AN EXPERT ON RARE BOOKS--ONE OF THE BEST. I SPECIALIZED IN **HANDWRITTEN** BOOKS, RATHER THAN FIRST EDITIONS.

BOOKS LIKE **ADELPHOE.** PUBLISHED BOOKS, BUT ONLY ONE COPY HAD EVER SEEN PRINT--A BIT LIKE A STILLBORN BABY.

ANYWAY, I AM--I **WAS** REALLY GOOD. FROM THE TYPES OF PAPER USED, TO CHANGES IN THE INKS OVER TIME, I COULD TELL **EVERYTHING** ABOUT A BOOK.

I COULD EVEN TELL HOW THE WEATHER WAS-- THE HUMIDITY IN THE ROOM--WHEN THE BOOK WAS BOUND. THEN, ONE DAY--

--THESE SHADY CHARACTERS SHOWED UP WITH A STOLEN BOOK. I TOLD THEM WHAT IT WAS WORTH, BUT THEN I CROSSED THE LINE: I FOUND A BUYER FOR IT.

MY BOSS EVENTUALLY FOUND OUT, AND I WAS FIRED. I DIDN'T KNOW WHAT TO DO UNTIL A FORMER CUSTOMER HELPED ME OUT.

HE'S A GREAT GUY, MR. HYDEN--A LEGITIMATE BUSINESSMAN. INTO FIRST EDITIONS OF EUROPEAN CLASSICS. ANYWAY, HE GAVE ME A JOB AS A FAVOR, EVEN THOUGH I KNOW NOTHING ABOUT HIS BUSINESS.

IT'S OKAY. YOU DON'T HAVE TO...

YOU DON'T HAVE TO TELL ME THE REST.

IF YOU PROMISE NOT TO TELL ANYONE, THERE'S A PLACE I'D LIKE TO SHOW YOU.

SO, WHERE ARE WE GOING?

TO THE ARCHIVES.

WHAT ARCHIVES?

ARCHIVES FULL OF UNWRITTEN BOOKS.

YOU MEAN HALF-WRITTEN MANUSCRIPTS?

NO, BOOKS. PRINTED BOOKS.

SO...

I DON'T GET IT.

BOOKS STILL BEING WRITTEN BY FAMOUS AUTHORS.

YOU'LL SEE. YOU'LL UNDERSTAND WHEN YOU SEE IT WITH YOUR OWN EYES.

HEY, GUILLERMO. HOW ARE YOU?

HELLO, MS. ANGELA.

HELLO TO YOU, TOO, SIR.

HOW DO YOU DO?

NOW, YOU HAVE TO PROMISE ME, OKAY? I'M SERIOUS.

YOU CAN'T TELL **ANYONE** ABOUT THIS PLACE! NO KIDDING, PETER--THERE WOULD BE **CONSEQUENCES.**

AND YOU CAN'T TAKE ANY BOOKS OUT OF HERE.

IF YOU TRY, IT'S NOT JUST *YOUR ASS* THAT'LL BE IN TROUBLE.

I MEAN *REAL* TROUBLE. REAL *DANGER.* I CAN TELL YOU'RE NOT TAKING ME SERIOUSLY.

KNOCK IT OFF, IT HURTS WHEN I LAUGH.

WELL, I CAN'T WAIT TO SEE YOUR FACE WHEN I OPEN THE DOOR.

HELLO, ANGELA.

HI, ESTELLE. HI, ARVORE. HOW ARE YOU LADIES TONIGHT?

BETTER, NOW THAT WINTER'S ALMOST OVER.

GOODBYE, NOW. HAVE A GOOD NIGHT.

GOOD NIGHT, DEAR. TAKE GOOD CARE OF YOURSELF.

PROMISE?

HUH? OH... YEAH... I PROMISE.

OKAY, THEN.

YOU ARE ABOUT TO ENTER ONE OF THE GREATEST WONDERS OF WORLD LITERATURE.

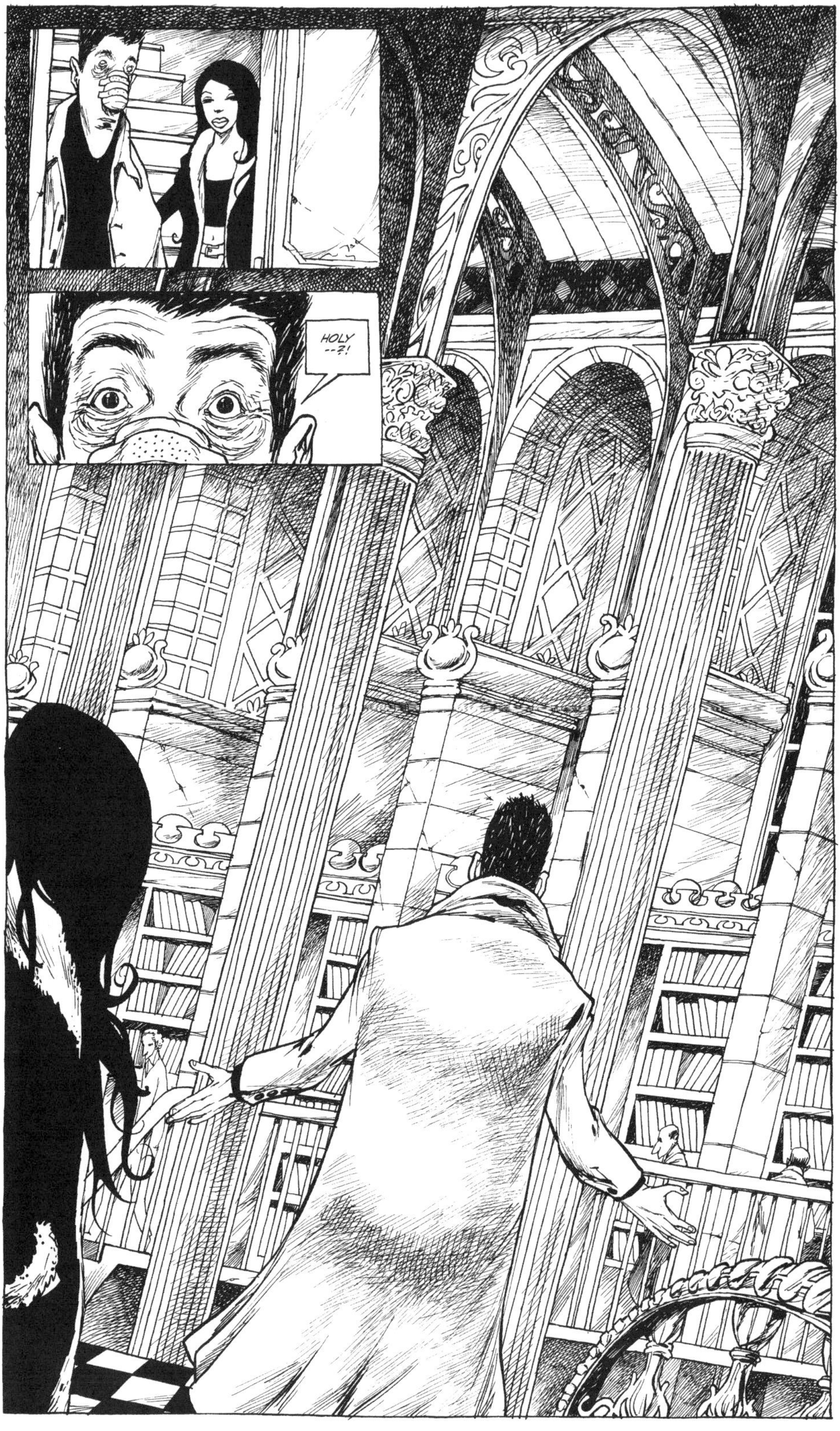
HOLY --?!

WHAT **IS** THIS?

SOME KIND OF **CANDID CAMERA** THING?

OKAY, YOU GOT ME. IT'S A TV SHOW, RIGHT?

NO, SIR, IT'S NOT!

WELCOME TO THE **ARCHIVES**.

C'MON, DON'T PULL MY LEG. WE WENT INTO A SMALL APARTMENT BUILDING, DOWN SOME STAIRS, AND THROUGH A NORMAL DOOR.

WE GOT IN HERE WITH A KEY.

HUSH! PLEASE BE QUIET.

THAT SEEMED **REAL**.

WALK WITH ME. YOU'LL GET IT SOON.

WHAT'S TO GET?

THAT THIS MIGHT BE THE BEST PLACE IN THE WHOLE **WORLD**.

HOLD IT. HOLD ON A SECOND. I'M GETTING A HEADACHE.

THE INSOMNIA AND ALL THOSE BLOWS TO THE HEAD... I'VE FINALLY LOST MY **MIND**.

ENOUGH ALREADY! YOU AND YOUR SELF-PITY. I THOUGHT YOU'D **LIKE** THIS PLACE.

41

GO! LOOK THROUGH THE BOOKS. SEE IF THEY'RE REAL.

SEE IF YOU'VE HEARD OF ANY OF THEM.

OKAY.

LET'S SAY IT'S ALL REAL. SOME WRITERS GAVE THEIR HALF-FINISHED BOOKS TO THEIR EDITORS AND PUBLISHED THEM. SO WHAT?

NO, NO, NO, NO!

NO PUBLISHER HAS THESE COPIES. *NO ONE* DOES.

SO THE WRITERS GAVE THEM TO THIS LIBRARY?

NO! SOME OF THEM MAY BE BEING WRITTEN AS WE SPEAK.

WHAT THE HELL ARE YOU *TALKING* ABOUT? ANYWAY, I DON'T HAVE MY GLASSES. HALF THESE BOOKS COULD BE EMPTY. MAYBE HALF THIS PLACE IS A PAINTING. HOW WOULD I KNOW?

FAIR ENOUGH. COME.

LOOK. TOUCH. THEY'RE ALL REAL.

SEE? ALL SALINGER. HE NEVER FINISHES HIS BOOKS.

HERE ARE ASIMOV'S BOOKS.

"BOOK." ONLY ONE.

WELL, HE WRITES FAST. IT MAY NOT BE HERE NEXT WEEK.

I'M SURE STEPHEN KING HAS ONE...

OKAY, I GET IT. THE ABORTION.

WHAT?

THE ABORTION. BRAUTIGAN'S NOVEL. THERE WAS A LIBRARY JUST LIKE THIS ONE IN THAT BOOK.

NO, NO, NOOO...

THAT WAS A PLACE WHERE PEOPLE TOOK THE ONLY COPY OF A BOOK THEY'D WRITTEN.

ALL THESE BOOKS ARE BEING WRITTEN RIGHT NOW.

THAT MAKES NO SENSE!

THEY'RE HALF-FINISHED, THEY AREN'T PUBLISHED, BUT THEY'RE IN A LIBRARY!

SIR?

WHEN YOU ENTERED THIS SMALL BUILDING, WERE YOU EXPECTING IT TO LEAD TO A PLACE LIKE THIS?

OF COURSE NOT. HOW COULD I?

AND YET, HERE YOU ARE.

YOU'RE STILL IN THE ARCHIVES, FOR NOW. WHEN YOU LEAVE, YOU WON'T BE HERE ANYMORE.

JUST LIKE THE BOOKS.

43

CHAPTER 5

DRILI
LILILI!
...

HELLO?

YES,
MR. OBLOMOV.
NO, SIR.
NOBODY
SHOWED UP.

IT'S 4:00 P.M. NOW. I TOOK OVER FOR SERGEI. HE WATCHED THE BUILDING OVERNIGHT.

WE ARE LOOKING EVERYWHERE! HE'S DISAPPEARED. NOT A *TRACE*.

YES, SIR. GOOD NIGHT.

SON OF A BITCH!

WHAT'S WRONG, SKIP?

THAT SON-OF-A-BITCH KOLINSKY. HE DOESN'T COME HOME, HE DOESN'T GO TO WORK. IT'S LIKE THE EARTH SWALLOWED THE MOTHERFUCKER UP.

I THOUGHT YOU GAVE THAT BOOK JOB TO SOMEONE ELSE.

OF COURSE I GAVE IT TO SOMEONE ELSE. I DON'T HAVE A *CONTRACT* WITH THAT ASSHOLE, DO I?

NO, SIR.

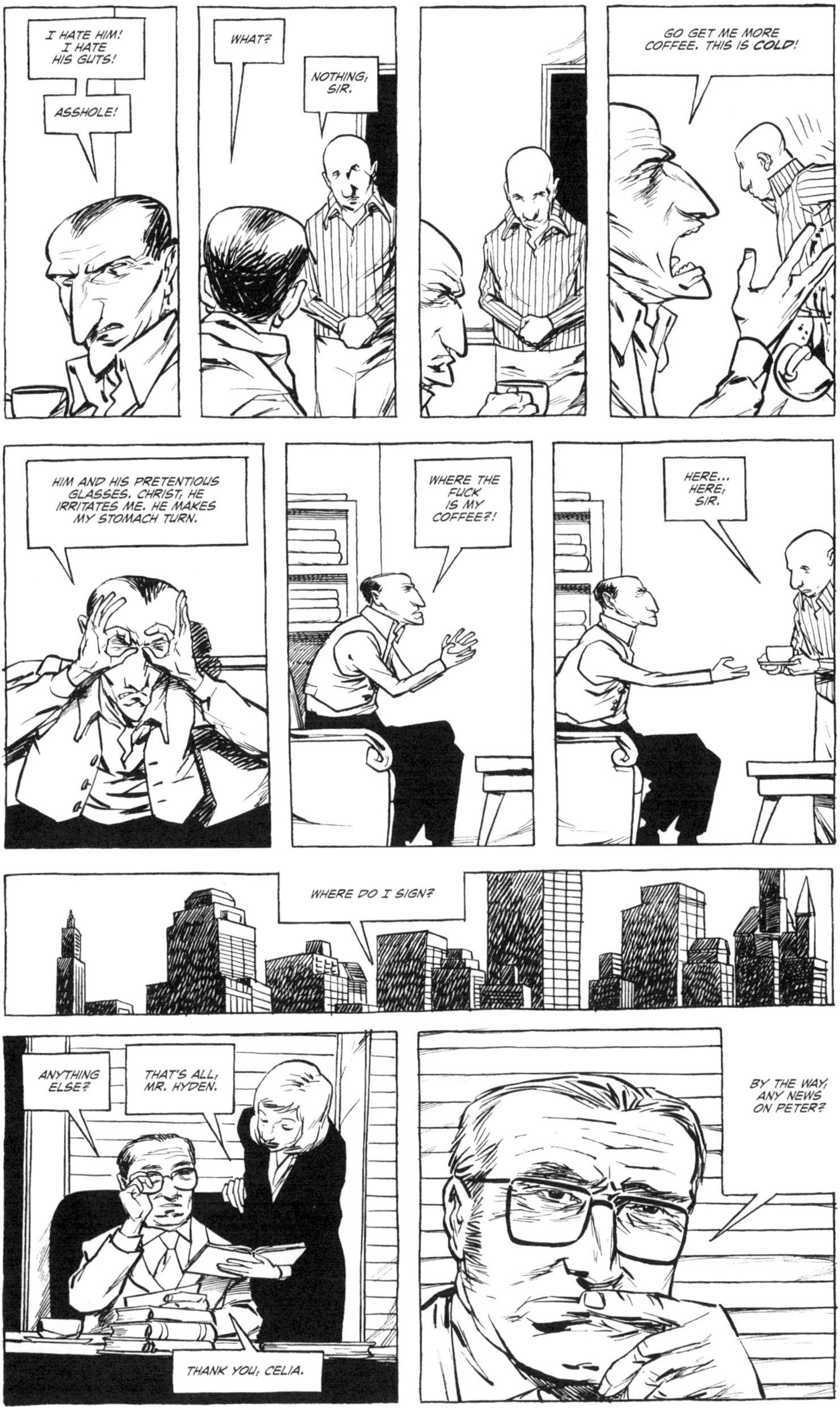
I HATE HIM! I HATE HIS GUTS!
ASSHOLE!
WHAT?
NOTHING, SIR.
GO GET ME MORE COFFEE. THIS IS **COLD**!
HIM AND HIS PRETENTIOUS GLASSES. CHRIST, HE IRRITATES ME. HE MAKES MY STOMACH TURN.
WHERE THE FUCK IS MY COFFEE?!
HERE... HERE, SIR.
WHERE DO I SIGN?
ANYTHING ELSE?
THAT'S ALL, MR. HYDEN.
THANK YOU, CELIA.
BY THE WAY, ANY NEWS ON PETER?

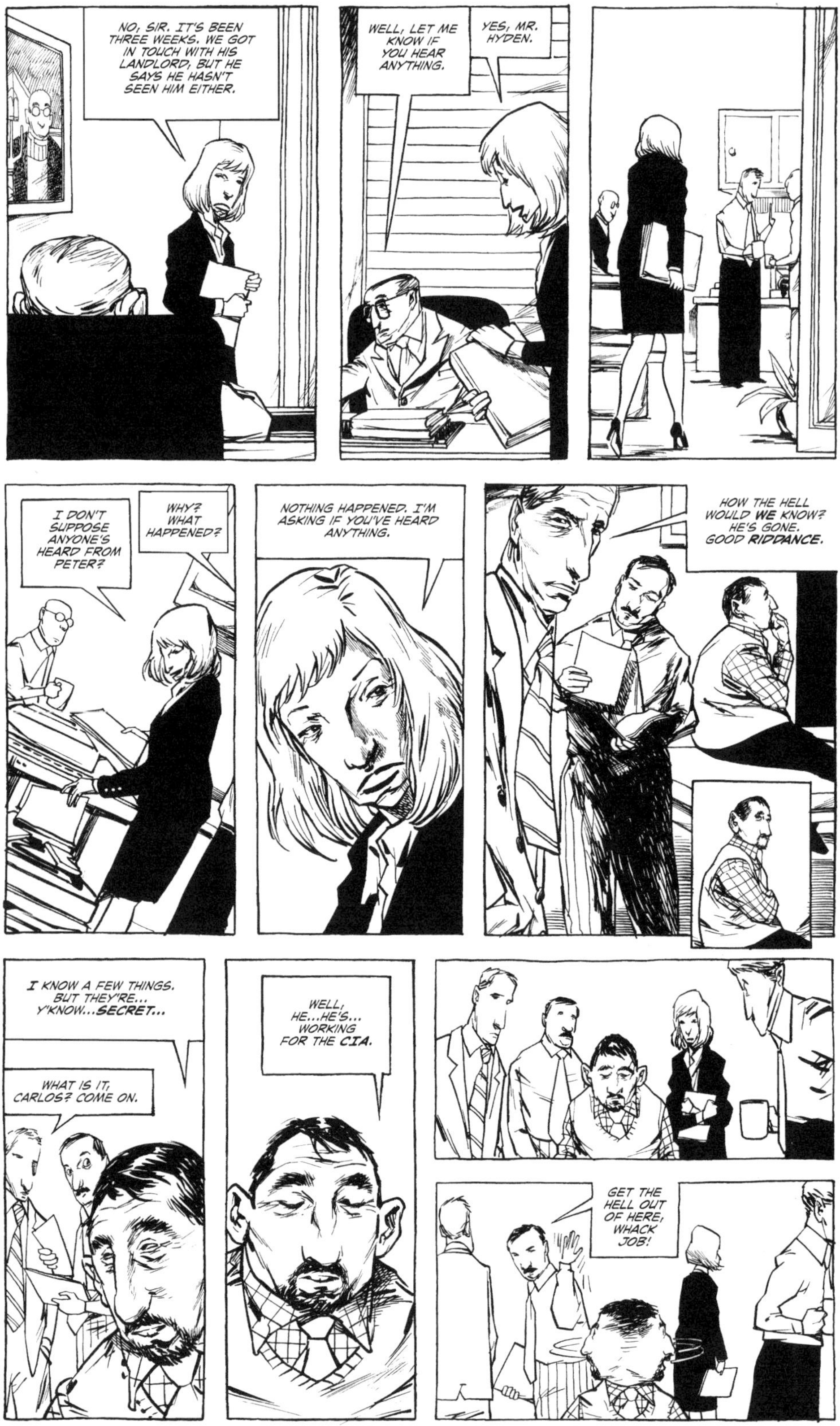
NO, SIR. IT'S BEEN THREE WEEKS. WE GOT IN TOUCH WITH HIS LANDLORD, BUT HE SAYS HE HASN'T SEEN HIM EITHER.
WELL, LET ME KNOW IF YOU HEAR ANYTHING.
YES, MR. HYDEN.
I DON'T SUPPOSE ANYONE'S HEARD FROM PETER?
WHY? WHAT HAPPENED?
NOTHING HAPPENED. I'M ASKING IF YOU'VE HEARD ANYTHING.
HOW THE HELL WOULD **WE** KNOW? HE'S GONE. GOOD **RIDDANCE**.
I KNOW A FEW THINGS. BUT THEY'RE... Y'KNOW...**SECRET**...
WHAT IS IT, CARLOS? COME ON.
WELL, HE...HE'S... WORKING FOR THE **CIA**.
GET THE HELL OUT OF HERE, WHACK JOB!

ENOUGH WITH YOUR SECRET AGENT BULLSHIT.

WAIT, NO... I SWEAR TO GOD.

TO HEAR YOU TELL IT, WE'RE ALL SPIES.

THE CLEANING LADY IS MOSSAD. EVEN MR. HYDEN IS CIA.

EXACTLY MY POINT. THAT'S HOW THEY KNOW EACH OTHER. WHY ELSE WOULD ANYONE HIRE KOLINSKY?

YOU KNOW WHAT, CARLOS? YOU NEED A GOOD SHRINK.

HE'S ALREADY GOT ONE.

ONE ISN'T ENOUGH. HE NEEDS AN ENTIRE INSTITUTE FOR THE CLINICALLY INSANE TO WORK ON HIM!

LIKE THE EUROPEAN ONES--OF THE LATE 1800s.

I REALLY WANT TO GO TO EUROPE SOMEDAY...

Insomnia

COFFEE SHOP

COFEE SHOP

EXCUSE ME, WAITER!

EXCUSE ME!

CAN WE GET THE CHECK?

I'LL BE RIGHT WITH YOU.

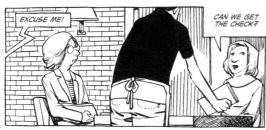

...AND JUST A LITTLE SUGAR, PLEASE.

SURE.

HE WORKS HARD.

HE'S A GOOD FIT FOR INSOMNIA CAFÉ.

SO...WHAT'S GOING ON?

WHERE?

BETWEEN YOU TWO.

NOTHING. HE NEEDED A JOB, I ASKED DAVID, DAVID SAID OKAY. THAT'S IT.

OH, C'MON!

"COME ON" WHAT? IF THERE **WERE** ANYTHING BETWEEN US, APRIL, D'YOU THINK I'D LET HIM SLEEP IN THE BACK OF THE COFFEE SHOP?

HEY, ANGELA.

HE-EY! WHAT'S UP?

I NEED ONE LATTE, ONE BAILEY'S AND COFFEE, AND A CHICKEN SALAD.

BAILEY'S AND COFFEE.

YOU HAVEN'T BEEN AROUND MUCH LATELY. I HEAR YOU'RE ONLY WORKING THREE DAYS A WEEK NOW.

YUP.

I'VE BEEN CHASING THIS OTHER JOB--AN OFFICE JOB, GOOD MONEY...THAT'D BE GREAT, Y'KNOW.

OH, SO... YOU'RE QUITTING SOON?

WELL, THIS ISN'T EXACTLY MY **DREAM** JOB.

MAYBE YOU'LL STILL STOP IN FOR COFFEE?

ASSHOLE.

CHAPTER
6

ANGELA, IF YOU DON'T NEED ME, I'M OUTTA HERE. SUN'S ALMOST UP.

GO AHEAD. I'LL CLOSE.

WE'RE GONNA GO SEE THIS STAND-UP COMIC. HE *DOES* *STAR WARS* ALL BY HIMSELF. WANNA COME?

NO THANKS. I'VE NEVER SEEN ANY OF THE *STAR TREK* OR *WARS* MOVIES. OR *JAWS*.

OR *RAMBO*. I GET IT.

'BY-EE, MR. K.

'BYE, MS. S.

IF *STAR WARS* IS OUT, GOT ANY OTHER PLANS TOMORROW?

WHY? YOU GOING TO INVITE ME TO THE NEW *HARRY POTTER* MOVIE?

HARRY POTTER? I'VE NEVER SEEN ONE OF THOSE MOVIES IN MY LIFE! OR *LORD OF THE RINGS*...

OR CHRONICLES OF NARNIA. OR--

I GET IT.

BUT I LIKE THE BOOKS. SPEAKING OF WHICH, HOW ABOUT WE PAY A VISIT TO THAT MAGICAL LIBRARY OF YOURS?

HUSH!

WHAT DID I TELL YOU? YOU'RE NOT SUPPOSED TO TALK ABOUT IT! I'VE ASKED YOU NOT TO--SEVERAL TIMES!

THERE'S NOBODY HERE. WHY ARE YOU SO UPSET?

YOU TALK TOO LOUD. WHAT IF SOMEBODY WALKS IN?

ALL RIGHT, ALL RIGHT. SORRY. BUT COME ON-- I'D LIKE TO TEST MY NEW GLASSES.

HMM. OKAY, BUT NOT FOR YOU. FOR YOUR GLASSES.

THANKS!

ALL RIGHT, GUYS, ALL THE FILES ARE EMAILED. I'M OFF.

THANKS, CARLOS. I'LL STICK AROUND A BIT, CHECK OUT THE NEW PROFILES ON MATCHME.COM.

HAVE A GOOD NIGHT, CELIA.

YOU TOO, CARLOS.

I *KNEW* IT! THAT SAME CAR'S BEEN THERE EVER SINCE PETER DISAPPEARED.

TELL ME THAT'S NOT *FISHY*. TELL ME THAT'S *NORMAL*. TELL ME THEY'RE JUST RANDOM PEOPLE. I KNEW IT! I *KNEW* IT!

PETER WAS MR. HYDEN'S BODYGUARD. PEOPLE GOT SUSPICIOUS, SO THE AGENCY PULLED HIM OUT AND REPLACED HIM WITH THE GUY IN THAT CAR.

PSST! CARLOS!

PETER?

HOLY SMOKE! WHERE THE HELL HAVE YOU BEEN?

HOW ARE YOU, MY FRIEND?

I'M FINE, WE'RE ALL FINE. HOW'S EVERYTHING WITH YOU? I SEE YOU'VE CHANGED YOUR GLASSES. FOR YOUR NEW MISSION, I ASSUME?

NEW MISSION?

AH, YES... FOR MY NEW MISSION.

I KNEW IT. I JUST SAW THE NEW GUY WHO'S REPLACED YOU.

WHAT NEW GUY?

THE AGENT STATIONED IN FRONT OF OUR BUILDING. TWO GUYS TAKE TURNS, BUT IT'S ALWAYS THE SAME CAR. THEY'RE BOTH TALL GUYS, LIKE YOU.

HE'S GOT HIS MEN HUNTING ME DOWN. IF THERE'S ONE THERE, THERE'LL DEFINITELY BE ANOTHER ONE AT MY HOUSE.

WHOSE MEN?

LISTEN, CARLOS, I NEED YOUR HELP. I HAVE SPARE KEYS AT THE OFFICE. I NEED YOU TO TAKE THEM AND GO TO MY PLACE.

YOU CAN COUNT ON MY DISCRETION.

IS...IS THIS...?

IS THIS A STATE MATTER?

OF COURSE! GO TO MY APARTMENT --SEE IF THERE'S ANYONE AROUND THE BUILDING OR IF SOMEONE'S BEEN IN THERE.

"STATE MATTER" ...YOU IDIOT.

CHAPTER 7

SORRY I'M A LITTLE LATE.

A *LITTLE?* WHEN YOU'RE LATE, YOU GO ALL OUT! AND HOW CAN YOU BE LATE FOR A JOB THAT STARTS AT 8:00 AT *NIGHT?* LET ALONE IN THE PLACE WHERE YOU LIVE!

I'M SORRY. I WAS LOOKING FOR AN APARTMENT.

OKAY. JUST DON'T BE LATE AGAIN, ALL RIGHT? THAT'S ALL I'M ASKING.

WHEREVER YOU WORK-- AN OFFICE OR A COFFEE SHOP--PEOPLE MAKE SUCH A BIG DEAL OVER THE SMALLEST STUFF.

HAVE A GOOD NIGHT, GUYS.

YOU LOOK DAPPER TODAY. HOT DATE?

NO, JUST SOME BUSINESS TO TAKE CARE OF.

C'MON, CARLOS. YOU CAN TELL ME. IS SHE KGB? MI6?

THERE'S NO GIRL, MAN. YOU KNOW THERE ARE MORE IMPORTANT ISSUES IN LIFE. FAR MORE *IMPORTANT* THAN OUR LITTLE LIVES.

TAXI!

CAN YOU PLEASE TAKE ME TO THIS ADDRESS?

HERE YOU GO, SIR.

DIT
DIT
DIT
DIT

MR. OBLOMOV-- LISTEN, THERE'S THIS WEIRD LITTLE GUY I'VE BEEN SEEING AT KOLINSKY'S OFFICE. I'M AT HIS APARTMENT RIGHT NOW--

--AND THE SAME GUY JUST SHOWED UP. HE'S HEADING TOWARD KOLINSKY'S BUILDING.

YES, SIR, I'M FOLLOWING HIM. HE'S GOING INTO THE BUILDING...GOT IT.

FIFTH FLOOR, THAT'S IT!

EXCUSE ME, I HAVE SOMETHING TO TELL YOU.

DON'T FUCKING **MOVE!** PUT YOUR HANDS UP, AND TURN AROUND.

NOW, I WANT SOME **ANSWERS.**

HAVE YOU GUYS HEARD ANYTHING FROM CARLOS? HE HASN'T SHOWN UP FOR **TWO** DAYS NOW.

WHO KNOWS? MAYBE THE CIA SENT HIM TO CZECHOSLOVAKIA! EVEN HIS MOTHER CALLED, LOOKING FOR HIM.

IT'S THE **CZECH REPUB-LIC.**

ALL RIGHT, GUYS... PLEASE LET ME KNOW IF YOU HEAR ANYTHING.

SO, NOW HE RAISES THE MONEY, RIGHT? BUT HE'S BLUFFING ...

MR. HYDEN? I'M SORRY, SIR.

YES, CELIA?

CARLOS MUÑOZ, THE LITTLE GUY IN ACCOUNTING, WITH THE GOATEE...HE DISAPPEARED A COUPLE OF DAYS AGO.

HE HASN'T BEEN HOME EITHER, AND HIS FAMILY'S WORRIED ABOUT HIM. ANYWAY--

--THE WEIRD THING IS, THE DAY HE DISAPPEARED, HE CAME TO MY DESK AND ASKED FOR KOLINSKY'S ADDRESS. HE SAID THAT PETER HAD ASKED HIM TO BRING OVER SOME OF HIS THINGS.

I DIDN'T KNOW THEY WERE FRIENDS. I DIDN'T THINK PETER **HAD** ANY FRIENDS IN THE OFFICE.

I DON'T THINK THEY **ARE** FRIENDS, SIR. THAT'S WHY I WAS SUSPICIOUS WHEN CARLOS ASKED FOR HIS ADDRESS.

PETER'S HOME ADDRESS? SURE, SURE. HOW **IS** PETER, BY THE WAY? I DIDN'T KNOW YOU GUYS WERE IN TOUCH. HE LEFT PRETTY SUDDENLY.

DON'T WORRY. HE'S OKAY.

THANKS A LOT. I SHOULD GO GET HIS STUFF **NOW**.

"THEN HE LEFT. I WAS CURIOUS, Y'KNOW--

"--SO I FOLLOWED HIM TO SEE WHAT WAS GOING ON.

"WE HAD ALREADY BOXED UP PETER'S BELONGINGS.

"HE WENT INTO PETER'S OFFICE AND STARTED GOING THROUGH THE BOX.

"THEN HE PULLED OUT A PAIR OF KEYS."

I'M PRETTY SURE THEY WERE KEYS TO PETER'S APARTMENT. ANYWAY, I DIDN'T ASK HIM ABOUT IT, BUT THEN THE NEXT DAY HE DIDN'T COME IN. SO, I THOUGHT MAYBE YOU'D WANT TO KNOW.

IT SOUNDS LIKE WE SHOULD CALL THE AUTHORITIES. TWO EMPLOYEES SUDDENLY DISAPPEARING LIKE THAT IS A MATTER FOR THE **POLICE**.

...YES, ANGELA, THE SECOND DRAFT LOOKS *MUCH* BETTER. YOU CAN START ON THE LAST FIVE CHAPTERS.

THANKS, HEIDI! I'LL EMAIL THE REVISION AS SOON AS POSSIBLE.

YOU'RE WELCOME, DEAR. STOP BY THE SIGNING ON FRIDAY.

OH, MY GOD! CAN I SEE YOUR PAPER FOR A MOMENT? PLEASE! IT'S VERY IMPORTANT.

HOLY SHIT!

SHIT!

SHIT!

Accountant Found Dead in Home of Missing Co-Worker

Carlos Muñoz, an accountant at a downtown book distribution company, was found dead of multiple gunshot wounds on Tuesday. Sources tell the Daily News that Muñoz sustained two shots to the head. Police are looking for the occupant of the apartment where Muñoz was found, Peter Kolinsky, who they say is the main suspect in the case.

Kolinsky, a former co-worker of Muñoz, has himself been missing for nearly two months.

CHAPTER 8

WHAT?

WHAT THE FUCK IS *THIS*?

YOU CAN'T POSSIBLY *BELIEVE* THIS, ANGELA. TELL ME YOU *DON'T*. HOW COULD *I KILL* SOMEONE?

OBLOMOV DID THIS. HE WAS TRYING TO GET ME *BACK* IN HIS DIRTY BUSINESS AGAIN. I REFUSED, AND I'VE BEEN HIDING FROM HIM. NOW HE'S DONE THIS TO *CORNER* ME!

HOLD IT! YOU ALWAYS USE THE SAME EXCUSE. "OBLOMOV COST ME MY *JOB*!" "OBLOMOV BROKE MY *NOSE*!" "I CAN'T GO TO WORK BECAUSE OF OBLOMOV'S *GOONS*!" "I CAN'T GO *HOME* BECAUSE OF *OBLOMOV*!" YOU SOUND LIKE THIS OBLOMOV GUY'S OUT TO RUIN YOUR LIFE!

I DON'T KNOW, PETER. WHAT WOULD *YOU* DO IF YOU WERE IN *MY* SHOES?

DON'T GET ME WRONG. I'M NOT SAYING YOU *DID* IT, BUT YOU HAVE TO ACCEPT THAT THIS WHOLE THING IS... DIFFICULT.

I ACCEPT THAT IT'S DIFFICULT FOR ME, BUT I CAN'T ACCEPT THAT IT'S DIFFICULT FOR YOU TO BELIEVE ME.

LOOK, PETER, I DON'T WANT TO GET INTO TROUBLE BECAUSE OF YOU. I GOT YOU A JOB, I GOT YOU A PLACE TO STAY...

EVERY CUSTOMER IN THIS CAFÉ KNOWS YOUR FACE, AND YOU KNOW THEY ALL READ THE PAPER. SOMEONE WILL RECOGNIZE YOU-- IT'S JUST A MATTER OF TIME. AND I'LL BURN WITH YOU.

WHAT ARE YOU SAYING?

I'M SAYING YOU NEED TO LEAVE. I'M SORRY.

ANGELA, THAT'S CRAZY TALK.

WHO'S CRAZY? IT'S UP TO THE POLICE NOW. THERE'S NOTHING ELSE I CAN DO BUT WISH YOU GOOD LUCK.

PLEASE, PLEASE... LEAVE BEFORE I OPEN THE CAFE.

IT'S OBLOMOV'S BROTHER. HE'S IN JAIL BECAUSE OF ME.

HE WENT TO PRISON BECAUSE OF A CLIENT I FOUND FOR THEM, A FRIEND OF A FRIEND. TURNS OUT THIS "FRIEND" WAS WORKING FOR THE COPS.

WHEN I MET HIM WITH THE BOOK, HE CAME WITH TWO OTHER GUYS-- UNDERCOVER COPS, WHO ASKED ME HOW I GOT THE BOOK. LIKE AN IDIOT, I TOLD THEM *EVERYTHING.*

I GAVE THEM THE NAME OF OBLOMOV'S BROTHER--HE WAS MY DIRECT CONTACT. THERE WAS A LOT OF MONEY AT STAKE. I WAS DISTRACTED.

ANYWAY, WHEN I FOUND OUT THEY WERE COPS, I TOLD THEM EVERYTHING--TO SAVE MY OWN ASS. BECAUSE I COOPERATED, THEY DIDN'T SEND *ME* TO JAIL, BUT I LOST MY JOB.

THEY GOT OBLOMOV'S BROTHER--AND *THAT'S* WHY OBLOMOV HATES MY GUTS.

I'M SORRY, PETER, BUT I DON'T WANT TO BE THE NEXT PERSON TO GO TO JAIL BECAUSE OF YOU. AND YOU CAN *COUNT* ON ME HATING YOU, TOO, IF THAT HAPPENS.

THE KEYS TO THE ARCHIVES. YOU WANT TO DROP ME LIKE A DIRTBAG, HUH? WE'LL SEE ABOUT THAT...

AT LEAST NOW I HAVE SOMEWHERE TO HIDE. BUT WHAT IF SOMEONE RECOGNIZES ME? WHAT AM I GOING TO DO?

WHAT IF I GO TO THE POLICE? TELL THEM EVERYTHING. TELL THEM I HAVE A WITNESS WHO WAS WITH ME WHEN THE MURDER TOOK PLACE.

"I CAN **PROVE** I WAS SOMEWHERE ELSE WHEN CARLOS WAS KILLED, OFFICER." "YEAH? WHERE **WERE** YOU?"

"I WAS IN THE **ARCHIVES.**" "YOU WERE IN THE ARCHIVES? **WHAT** ARCHIVES?"

"IT'S THIS PLACE WHERE THERE'S A COPY OF EVERY BOOK THAT'S BEING WRITTEN AT THE MOMENT."

"WELL, WHY DIDN'T YOU SAY SO? YOU'RE FREE TO GO! HE'S **CLEAN**, COMMISSIONER. HE WAS IN THE **ARCHIVES.**"

DRILILILILILILI

HELLO?

PETER?

WHAT EXPLANATION?

MR. HYDEN, I KNOW YOU HAVE NO REASON TO BELIEVE **ANYTHING** I TELL YOU, BUT I'M BEGGING YOU TO LISTEN TO ME ONE LAST TIME.

NO, NO, NO...YOU LISTEN TO *ME*. I TREATED YOU LIKE A *SON*, AND WHAT DID YOU DO IN RETURN? YOU KEPT *LYING*. WHY SHOULD I BELIEVE *ANYTHING* YOU SAY, YOU CUNNING BASTARD? I SAW YOU GIVE YOUR DEPARTMENT CHIEF A FAKE NAME FOR YOUR *DENTIST*, OF ALL THINGS! YOU THINK YOU'RE THE *ONLY* ONE WHO KNOWS ANY TRIVIA?

B.H. McKEEBY WAS GRANT WOOD'S DENTIST. HE'S THE GUY WHO POSED FOR "AMERICAN GOTHIC." YOU'RE NOT JUST A REGULAR LIAR, YOU'RE *PATHOLOGICAL*. YOU ENJOY MAKING PEOPLE LOOK *STUPID* WITH YOUR LIES.

YOU *BAIT* THEM TO SEE IF THEY'RE AS SMART AS YOU.

WELL, *I'M* NOT AS STUPID AS YOU THINK.

I NEVER THOUGHT YOU WERE.

"NEVER, EVER--"

"--IGNORE A MAN'S COURTESY."

YOU CAN WRITE THAT ON THE WALLS OF YOUR CELL...

...YOU MURDERING PRICK!

I'M TOTALLY FUCKED. OKAY, RELAX...FIRST THING, I NEED A BRIEFCASE. THEN I'LL GO TO THE ARCHIVES.

I'LL TAKE A SALINGER TO BRING TO OBLOMOV, EXPLAIN TO HIM HOW VALUABLE IT IS. MAYBE EVEN HOOK HIM UP WITH A BUYER.

IT'LL BE EASIER TO CONVINCE HIM THAT WAY. IF I'M GOING TO STAY OUT OF PRISON, I'LL NEED CASH TO ESCAPE.

AND THAT WHORE'LL GET IN TROUBLE BECAUSE SHE LET ME INTO THE ARCHIVES IN THE FIRST PLACE. THIS ALL STARTED WHEN I MET HER, ANYWAY. THAT COFFEE SHOP!

GOOD EVENING, LADIES. MY NAME IS **DETECTIVE TONY BARTELLA.** I HAVE A COUPLE QUESTIONS REGARDING ONE OF YOUR EMPLOYEES.

Insomni

I'M SURE YOU SAW THE PAPERS. HIS NAME IS *PETER KOLINSKY.*

YES, DETECTIVE, I SAW THE PAPERS, BUT I HAVEN'T SEEN PETER SINCE YESTERDAY. WHAT HAPPENED TO YOUR EYE?

AS THEY SAY, YOU SHOULD SEE THE OTHER GUY. I UNDERSTAND KOLINSKY *LIVES* HERE AS WELL. PLEASE LET ME KNOW IF HE SHOWS UP--

--OR IF SOMEONE COMES IN TO PICK UP HIS STUFF. AND I DON'T APPRECIATE THAT SARCASTIC SMILE. WE'RE INVESTIGATING A *MURDER* HERE.

"WHAT HAPPENED TO YOUR EYE?" YOU'RE CRAZY! I THOUGHT HE WAS GOING TO **ARREST** YOU.

I **LOVE** ITALIANS.

SO, WHAT DO YOU THINK? DID PETER REALLY DO IT?

I...I THINK HE'S GOT A LOT OF PROBLEMS. EVEN IF HE **DIDN'T** KILL THAT POOR GUY, IT HAPPENED **BE-CAUSE** OF HIM. HE'S SO WEIRD, APPEALING, AND **IRRITATING** AT THE SAME TIME. THAT'S WHY I WANTED TO USE HIM IN MY NOVEL.

EXCUSE ME, LADIES. I SAW THAT WAITER IN THE PAPER--PETER, I BELIEVE HIS NAME WAS. DO YOU HAVE A PICTURE OF HIM HERE? I'D LOVE TO PUT IT IN MY ARCHIVES.

GOOD EVENING, GUILLERMO.

GOOD EVENING, SIR. I THINK MS. ANGELA'S AT WORK.

I KNOW. THAT'S WHY I'M HERE. SHE SENT ME TO PICK UP A FEW THINGS FOR HER. SEE YOU LATER.

OKAY, KEYS TO THE ARCHIVES. WORK FAST, AND ACT NORMAL.

C'MON, STRAIGHT AHEAD TO THE "S" SECTION.

WAIT FOR THIS GUY TO PICK A BOOK.

JESUS, I'VE NEVER FELT LIKE THIS BEFORE. MY HEART IS BEATING A MILE A MINUTE... RELAX, PETER, RELAX!

ACT *NORMAL*. YOU'RE AN AVID READER. YOU'RE CURIOUS TO SEE IF THERE ARE ANY NEW PAGES BY YOUR FAVORITE WRITER. YOU HAVEN'T *STOLEN* ANYTHING. YET.

I WISH I DIDN'T HAVE MY GLASSES ON--LIKE THE FIRST TIME I WAS HERE. I'D PROBABLY BE LESS NERVOUS.

IT WOULD BE SO MUCH EASIER TO GO THROUGH WITH THIS IF I DIDN'T HAVE TO FOCUS ON ANYTHING OR SEE IF ANYONE WAS LOOKING AT ME.

ALL RIGHT, APRIL, I'M HEADING HOME. I HAVE TO GET UP IN A COUPLE HOURS. CAN YOU LOCK UP BY YOURSELF?

SURE. GO AHEAD.

I'M SO TIRED. I CAN'T WAIT UNTIL I'M OUT OF THIS DUMP FOR GOOD.

THEN GO HOME, AND GOOD LUCK WRITING.

'BYE, HONEY.

I WONDER IF THEY'LL EVER COME UP WITH SOME KIND OF VISUAL SILENCER FOR GUNS. LIKE A REGULAR SILENCER, BUT FOR THE MUZZLE FLASH.

DON'T LEAVE RIGHT AWAY. SIT HERE A LITTLE LONGER. READ THE BOOK QUIETLY. NO SUDDEN MOVES.

I SHOULD GO NOW. IT'S LATE, AND I FEEL SLEEPY. OKAY, DON'T GO DIRECTLY TO THE EXIT. TAKE IT SLOW. I'LL SPEND THE NIGHT IN A PARK OR SOMETHING, THEN CALL OBLOMOV FIRST THING IN THE MORNING.

UHH...

LAIKA! SHUT UP! BAD DOG!

WOOF! WOOF! WOOF!

LEAVE THE HOMELESS MAN ALONE.

MY HEAD...

"HOMELESS"? I GUESS HE'S *TECHNICALLY* RIGHT... UGHHH... BETTER CLEAR MY HEAD BEFORE THE BIG DAY. COFFEE...

EXCUSE ME, SIR?

MR. KOLINSKY? PETER? MAY WE HAVE A WORD WITH YOU?

IT'S ABOUT A CERTAIN OBJECT. WE'D LIKE YOU TO ACCOMPANY US TO A PLACE OF MUTUAL INTEREST.

" ...PLACE"? WHO *ARE* THESE GUYS? NOT COPS, SO... SHIT! HOW DID THEY FIND ME SO QUICKLY?

HEY! STOP!

IT'S BLEEDING? HOW IS THAT **POSSIBLE?** OH, MY GOD...

POLICE! OPEN THE DOOR!

UH...

UH...HOLD ON A SECOND.

OPEN THE GODDAMN DOOR **NOW!**

I JUST NEED A MOMENT. I'M ... USING THE BATHROOM.

OKAY, I'M UNLOCKING THE DOOR NOW. WHAT'S THE PROBLEM?

HANDS WHERE WE CAN SEE THEM! DON'T DO ANYTHING STUPID!

SIR, STEP OUT THE DOOR. **NOW.** KEEP YOUR HANDS UP.

ALL RIGHT, ALL RIGHT.

GET HIM AGAINST THE WALL. SEE WHAT'S IN THE BRIEFCASE.

DON'T MOVE!

IF THIS IS ABOUT THE TOILET, I WAS GOING TO FLUSH.

SHUT UP.

TAKE A LOOK AROUND. SEE IF THERE'S ANYTHING ELSE.

CHAPTER 9

SHE'S CONSCIOUS, BUT PLEASE BE CAREFUL. CONSIDER THE MENTAL STATE SHE'S IN.

AND I CAN'T ALLOW YOU *BOTH* IN, DETECTIVE. ONLY ONE VISITOR AT A TIME. PLEASE TRY TO KEEP IT SHORT.

THANK YOU, DOCTOR. WHILE DETECTIVE BARTELLA IS WITH HER, CAN I ASK YOU A COUPLE QUESTIONS?

HELLO, ANGELA. I'M VERY SORRY ABOUT WHAT HAPPENED.

HI, DETECTIVE. YOUR EYE IS BETTER.

I KNOW IT'S VERY DIFFICULT, BUT I HAVE TO ASK YOU A COUPLE OF THINGS. WE CAN STOP WHENEVER YOU WANT. ALL RIGHT?

I THINK I CAN HANDLE IT. WHATEVER HAPPENED, HAPPENED. I'LL TELL YOU EVERYTHING I KNOW. THAT NIGHT YOU CAME TO THE CAFÉ, PETER *HAD* SHOWN UP EARLIER. I KICKED HIM OUT, EVEN THOUGH I DIDN'T REALLY BELIEVE HE'D KILLED THAT GUY. IN A WAY, MAYBE I WAS TRYING TO PROTECT HIM, Y'KNOW, UNTIL THE CASE GOT SOLVED.

WHEN YOU SHOWED UP, I DIDN'T REALIZE HOW SERIOUS THE WHOLE SITUATION STILL WAS. I LEFT THE CAFÉ AROUND 5:00 A.M. I WAS TIRED, SO APRIL WAS GOING TO CLOSE UP.

"I HAD A MEETING WITH MY EDITOR LATER IN THE DAY, SO I NEEDED SOME SLEEP.

"WHEN I GOT TO MY BUILDING, I REALIZED I DIDN'T HAVE MY KEYS.

"I RANG THE SUPER, GUILLERMO, AND ASKED HIM FOR THE SPARE KEY. HE LOOKED SUSPICIOUS FOR A MOMENT. I THOUGHT MAYBE HE WAS JUST SLEEPY. THEN HE SAID:"

BUT, MS. ANGELA, YOUR FRIEND WITH THE GLASSES CAME BY AND TOLD ME YOU ASKED HIM TO GRAB A COUPLE THINGS FOR YOU. I DIDN'T SEE HIM LEAVE AFTERWARDS.

GLASSES? YOU MEAN PETER? ARE YOU SURE? I DIDN'T ASK HIM TO COME HERE. HOW DID HE GET MY KEYS?

OF COURSE I'M SURE. I THOUGHT IT WAS STRANGE, TOO, BUT I FIGURED IT WAS NONE OF MY BUSINESS.

WELL, ANYWAY, I'LL SEE IF HE'S STILL HERE.

NO, MS. ANGELA, THIS SOUNDS A BIT WEIRD. I'LL COME WITH YOU. LET ME PUT SOMETHING ON.

THANKS, GUILLERMO. I APPRECIATE IT.

"WE WENT UPSTAIRS. I STILL WASN'T VERY WORRIED. I WAS A LITTLE UNEASY, BUT NOT REALLY SCARED.

"WE FOUND MY DOOR OPEN. I THOUGHT MAYBE PETER HAD GONE IN AND STOLEN SOMETHING. PROBABLY MY MANUSCRIPT, TO HURT ME."

HELLO... PETER? PETER, ARE YOU HERE?

HE MUST HAVE LEFT ALREADY. I SHOULD CALL THE COPS, OR MAYBE JUST GET SOME SLEEP.

LET'S LOOK AROUND FIRST, TO MAKE SURE HE'S GONE.

THUD!

NG...

STILL WANT TO CALL THE COPS? IT'S A LITTLE LATE NOW.

P-PETER... WHAT THE HELL ARE YOU DOING?

YOU DID KILL THAT GUY, DIDN'T YOU? WHAT DO YOU WANT FROM ME? ALL I EVER DID WAS HELP YOU.

I DIDN'T KILL HIM, YOU IDIOT! I TOLD YOU-- AND YOU DIDN'T HELP ME. YOU USED ME!

IN A WAY, PETER WAS RIGHT. I'M WRITING A BOOK ABOUT INSOMNIA--THAT'S WHY I WAS WORKING AT THE CAFÉ. WHEN I MET HIM, I KNEW HE WAS PERFECT FOR MY BOOK. HE KNEW ABOUT IT, AND WE TALKED ABOUT HIS CASE.

CRAZY AS THIS SOUNDS, I HAVE TO BRING IT UP. HE TOLD US A STORY ABOUT YOU TAKING HIM TO A PLACE CALLED "THE ARCHIVES," WHICH HAD BOOKS THAT WERE IN THE PROCESS OF BEING WRITTEN BY FAMOUS AUTHORS. DID HE EVER MENTION ANYTHING LIKE THAT TO YOU?

"THE ARCHIVES"? THAT'S WHAT I'VE BEEN CALLING ALL THE RESEARCH I HAVE AT HOME. MY NOTES, MY BOOKS, PHOTO ALBUMS, ALL THAT...

HE WANTED TO READ MY BOOK, BUT I TOLD HIM IT WAS A SECRET. I DIDN'T WANT PEOPLE AT THE CAFÉ TO KNOW I WAS WRITING ABOUT THEM.

APRIL, THE OTHER GIRL AT THE CAFÉ--**SHE** KNEW ABOUT IT. SHE'S AN OLD FRIEND OF MINE. THE OWNER KNEW, TOO. HE'S A FRIEND OF MY EDITOR.

I THOUGHT PETER WAS OUR MOST INTERESTING CUSTOMER, FULL OF STORIES AND A STRANGE PAST. AFTER EVERYTHING HE TOLD ME, I FELT LIKE I OWED HIM THE TRUTH. SO I TOLD HIM ABOUT MY BOOK. I TOOK HIM HOME AND CALLED IT "THE ARCHIVES."

HE CAME ALONG WITH ME A FEW MORE TIMES BECAUSE HE WANTED TO READ MY BOOK. I WRITE BY HAND, LIKE VIRGINIA WOOLF. I TYPE IT LATER FOR MY EDITOR. HE WANTED TO READ THE HANDWRITTEN MANUSCRIPT.

SINCE HE'S AN EXPERT ON OLD HANDWRITTEN BOOKS, I THOUGHT IT WAS AMUSING-- A LITTLE ROMANTIC ON HIS PART. MAYBE I FELT A SECRET PRIDE ABOUT IT, TOO. I DON'T KNOW.

I NEVER LIKED HIM, TO TELL YOU THE TRUTH. NOT AS A **REAL** PERSON, ANYWAY. I LIKED HIM AS A FICTIONAL CHAR- ACTER. I DIDN'T REALLY BELIEVE HE COULD KILL SOMEONE, BUT MAYBE HE COULD KEEP IT A SECRET IF HE KNEW SOME- ONE WHO DID.

HE DIDN'T KILL CARLOS. WE KNOW WHO DID IT AND WHO ORDERED IT. NOT EVERYTHING HE TOLD YOU--OR US--WAS A LIE. ACTUALLY, THERE WAS SOME TRUTH TO IT ALL. IT WAS JUST WARPED IN HIS MIND. HE DIDN'T SAY THOSE THINGS TO DECEIVE PEOPLE--HE WAS DECEIVING HIMSELF.

SO OBLOMOV EXISTS. BUT IT'S PROBABLY NOT HIS **REAL** NAME, RIGHT? I DOUBT SOME MAFIA GUY GAVE HIMSELF THAT NAME. HE DOESN'T SOUND LIKE SOMEONE WHO READS GONCHAREV; BUT PETER DOES. I FEEL GUILTY, DETECTIVE. I FEEL LIKE I DECEIVED HIM, TOO.

YOU *USED* ME, LIKE EVERYONE ELSE IN MY LIFE. IT'S ALWAYS MY *EXPERTISE* IN SOMETHING THAT COUNTS, NOT *ME*. NOBODY FEELS AFFECTION FOR ME--JUST GUILT.

PETER, I'M YOUR FRIEND.

YOU WANT ME TO *THINK* YOU'RE MY FRIEND. YOU WANT TO BE MY FRIEND *NOW* BECAUSE YOU'RE IN TROUBLE. YOU DIDN'T WANT TO BE FRIENDS WHEN *I* WAS IN TROUBLE.

"THE LAST THING I REMEMBER IS HIM RAISING THE BRONZE ELEPHANT STATUE. THEN...THEN I WOKE UP HERE, WITHOUT MY HANDS. THAT WAS HIS REVENGE. HE TOOK MY HANDS AND MY BOOK."

ANGELA...UM...I'M GOING TO LET YOU REST A LITTLE NOW. I'M SORRY I HAD TO MAKE YOU GO THROUGH ALL THIS AGAIN.

IT'S OKAY, DETECTIVE. JUST TELL ME WHAT TIME IT IS.

THE TIME?

IT'S... UM...

IT'S 3:30. TRY TO GET SOME SLEEP, ANGELA. GOODBYE.

HOW IS SHE?

HOW CAN SHE BE? KOLINSKY'S GOING TO SPEND THE REST OF HIS LIFE IN AN INSTITUTION; AND SHE'S GOING TO SPEND HERS NEEDING ONE.

MAN, THIS IS FUCKED UP. THIS REALLY IS ONE FOR THE BOOKS.

LET'S GET OUT OF HERE. I NEED A CUP OF COFFEE.

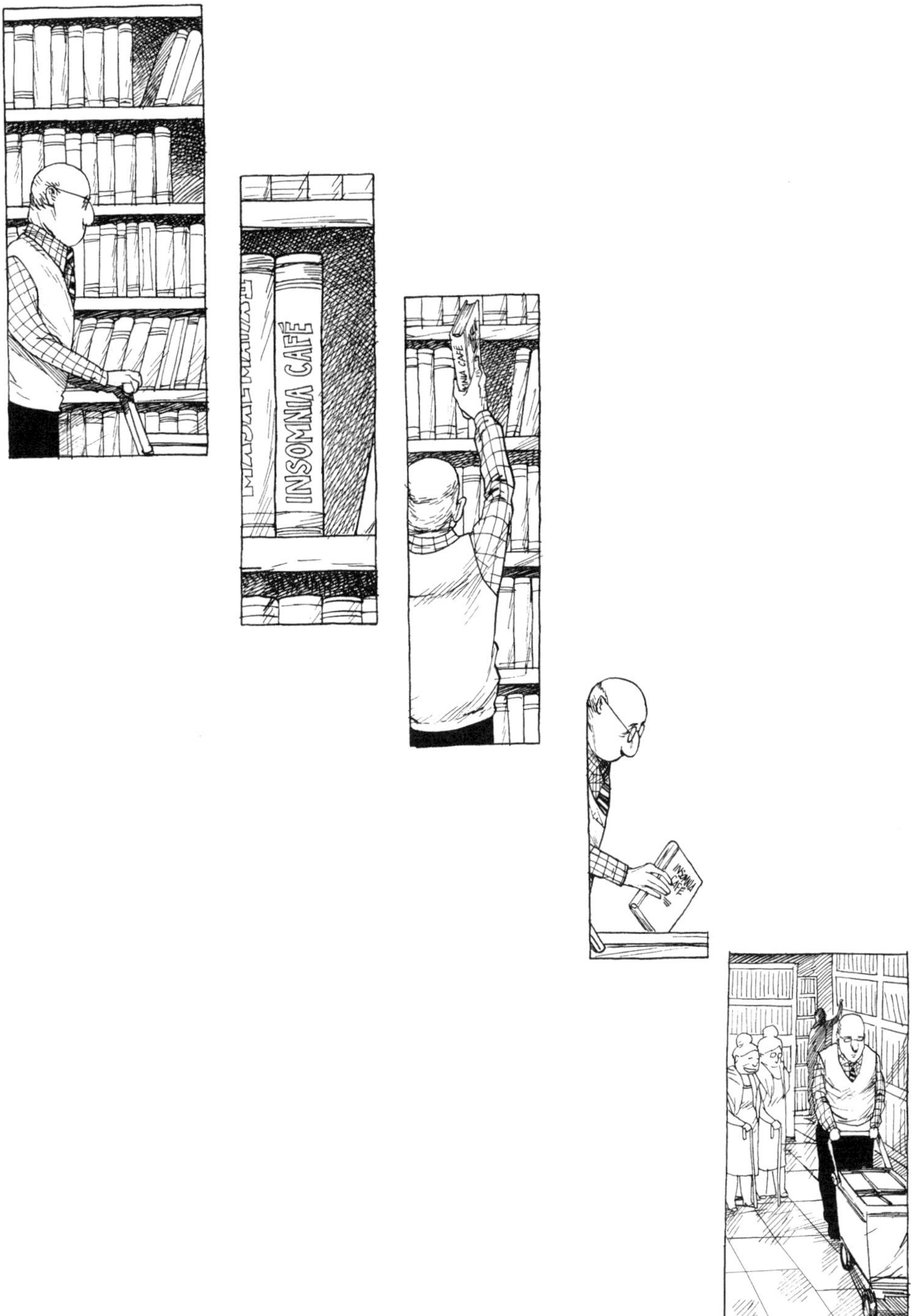
INSOMNIA CAFÉ
INSOMNIA CAFÉ

ABOUT THE AUTHOR:

M. K. PERKER was born in Istanbul, Turkey, in 1972 and has gone on to become one of Turkey's most prominent illustrators, working as both an editorial cartoonist and comics artist. In Turkey he has published the graphic novels *Türkan Şoray Dudağı* and *Masal Mafya*.

In recent years, Perker has found similar success in the United States, providing illustrations for publications such as *The New York Times*, *The Wall Street Journal*, *The New Yorker*, *Mad Magazine*, *Heavy Metal*, and *The Progressive*. His American comics work includes *Cairo* and the Eisner-nominated series *Air*, both written by G. Willow Wilson and published by Vertigo, as well as contributions to Dark Horse's *Noir* and *Escapist* anthologies.

Perker currently lives and works in New York City, where he is the first Turkish member of the Society of Illustrators.

Photo by Baris Acarli